Words to Her

Rocky Ramirez

authorHOUSE®

AuthorHouse™
1663 Liberty Drive
Bloomington, IN 47403
www.authorhouse.com
Phone: 833-262-8899

Published by AuthorHouse 02/23/2022

ISBN: 978-1-6655-5305-6 (sc)
ISBN: 978-1-6655-5304-9 (e)

Library of Congress Control Number: 2022903613

Print information available on the last page.

You've always been a better person than I.
That's why I was so drawn to you.
Being around you made me better.
And that's why I dedicate this to you,
And why I dedicate the rest of my life
To being better.

I loved so many,
But there was one I truly loved,
And I had forgotten who the many were.

It's been twenty-one days.
And I still miss you.

You would cry and tremble
When we made love.
That, I will never forget.
Our passion might have been mistaken for love.
But it was the best love that wasn't real,
A love I struggle to repeat over and over.

Minutes before I caught her cheating,
She sent me a text that said,
"Just finished 9 chapters."
Damn!

Ruthless

To the ones who made us.

There are days I start to miss you.
Then I open my eyes.

Miserable

I could continue faking happiness and
Living miserably.
Just live miserably.
Living miserably was easier.

My heart is empty
Now that you're gone.
It feels faintly
Now that we're done.

She was as beautiful as fire.
And just as dangerous.

To be told you're not enough
Is nothing close
To being shown
You never were.

All the leaves have changed colors.
The smells of pinon now burn in the night air.
You left me so damn suddenly
With this dark emptiness to now bear.

Dear self,
Today has been a really hard day.
I know you want to seclude yourself till you end
The sadness and unhappiness.
But remember,
The gloom will end, and the sun will shine again.
You will smile, and your heart will beat as it once did.

I loved her so much
Because she was just like me.
We would never work, though,
Because I hated who I was.

The texts got less, and the visits got shorter.
No more sweet kisses, and your distance got further.

That spark was gone, but I was determined to reignite.
But I failed us both; you were no longer in the fight.

The love I yearned for, just like you gave me before,
You decided was for others and that I deserved to mourn.

You strung me along like an injured fly in your web.
You waited for me to give up, and now I am dead.

I did my best writings,
Had my best thoughts
When my heart was in pain.
Kind of like when a garden blossoms better
After a long, hard rain.

My Love

We loved, and we laughed together.
We battled like vicious storms.
I loved how you wore your halo,
How it covered your sharpened horns.

She wonders why you are how you are.
Dead, cold, and silent.
Maybe it's because years ago,
She took your heart and crushed it.

Do you want to know what pain is?
Make sweet love to your wife after
not seeing her for months.
She then turns to you with tears in her eyes and says,
"I want a divorce. I slept with someone else."

The Bar

Lonesome bar for a lonesome man.
A few lone strangers,
One serving bartender with a simple name, Stan.

Pouring of a long, strong drink
Into a hollow, empty glass
To drink away their sorrows,
To annihilate their pasts.

The musky dust all settled in this old-
fashioned barroom.
Lonesome country music plays in the distance,
And its sadness consumes.

The Next Day

You have lost her for good.
Realize it, and just accept it.
Now sleep as much as you can.
Let your pain die; let it quit.

Eventually you will realize it is time
To wake up and finally live.
Mourn your loss, pieces picked.
Move on and just forgive.

Your Worth

There are moments in time
When you realize you're now nothing
But a part of her past,
No longer worth loving.

She laughs at the thought of you
Hurting and suffering.
The pillow to your face,
You're only worth smothering.

The Ledge

You were created to be able to talk
People off the ledge.
But you won't be able
To talk yourself off.

Picked

You said I didn't love you enough to leave.
You said I didn't love you enough to pick you.

But if you loved me enough, like you said you did,
You would have waited, or you would have left me before
You messed around with three other men.

So neither of us picked shit.

Have you ever been so loved
And so hated by the same person?

I sit alone in my heart,
Waiting for you to show.
My mind just keeps running,
Where are you? Who knows?

I miss my boo,
But she's so long gone.
I sit on my karma
Because of what I did wrong.

I begged for the bare minimum in the end.
The tables have turned, and to hell
My heart she did send.

You wake up one day and realize
Everybody loves you,
But nobody really likes you.

I've done everything I've wanted to do
In life up to this point.
Except one thing.
And I think my chances for that
Are long gone
Because you're gone.

When you lose someone very important to you in your life,
You begin to feel as if you're dying every second.
They were that important to your existence.

The drugs aren't working anymore.
The scars to my wounds won't stay closed.

No one likes me,
And that's OK.
I don't like myself either.

I wanted it to be you.
I wanted it to be you so bad.
But you didn't want it to be me.

I would do anything for you
To check in on me,
Ask me if I'm OK
So I can reply to you,
"No, no I'm not."

People keep asking me,
"Is there is any chance you'll get back together again?"
I simply have to say,
"I don't know."

In Love with a Zombie

The last two years have felt like I've been loving a zombie.
You're there,
But you're dead inside,
Just slowly eating my brains and my heart.

It was to be you.
It was supposed to be us.

I had destroyed her spirit.
I had aged her soul.
When I was dying,
She repaired me whole.

I hurt her deeply.
I scarred her soul.
She was a beautiful queen,
But I had taken her whole.

I hate myself
For killing her slowly.
I ask the man upstairs to
Strike me quickly.

Nothing makes sense without you.

You didn't have to run
To all those other guys.
But after talking to my therapist,
I now know why.

You needed validation
That someone would want you.
I actually chose you a long time ago,
But 100 percent I could not do.

I'm not mad at you,
Just truly devastated.
I asked for way too much.
It's my fault your love faded.

I swore to you
That you would be the last woman I would ever love.
And now that you're gone,
I've kept that promise.

My son asked me one day,
"Dad, have you ever been in love?"
You were the first to pop up in my head.
He then asked me,
"Dad, have you ever had your heart broken?"
You were the first to pop up in my head.

If I knew that day would be the last day
That I would ever feel you,
I would never have let you go.

Meeting the right person at the wrongest time
was the hardest thing I will ever have to realize in life.

I know someday I'll just be a memory to you.
I hope that it will at least be a great one.

She's precious and beautiful.
This you'll always see.
Every now and then take a break,
And take her to the ocean, the sea.

Don't take her for granted
Just like I once did.
You'll live with regret,
And every day you'll feel sick.

Love her tight, like
You might lose her tomorrow.
Every day is not guaranteed.
A redo you can't borrow.

Quit lying to my heart.
Quit telling me I still love her.
You are only mine;
You are not hers.

Do right by me,
Not like she didn't.
Convince me what my brain tells me,
And hate her for eternity.

We did all that love and life
To become strangers again in the end.

If I truly had the chance to redo it—
Go back in time and meet you once again—
Would I?
Absolutely!
Every single time.
But make it even better.

My Valentine

I love you on this day they call Valentine's.
But I'll love you every day they call today.

Come Back

A second doesn't go by
That I don't want to beg for you to come back.
I just needed you to know that.

A Grand Gesture

She always wanted a grand gesture from me—
To fight for her,
To choose her.

But that's something I just couldn't do,
Even though I tried in my mind
Over and over.

I should have jumped
And taken that chance.
I should have run to her, grabbed her,
And forever just danced.

I should have just showed up.

Keep Breathing

What do you do
When your lungs tell you to keep breathing,
But your heart tells you
That it's time to stop?

All I wanted was peace with her.
All we had was war till the end.

It's so cold and dark alone.

I reflect on all the bad things you did to me.
No enemy would have done the things you did.
But I still need you.
I still want you.
I still love you.

The women I had an affair with once asked me,
"Why did you marry someone so ugly?"
And I replied,
"And we're not?"

Today

Today I miss her.
Today I still remember.

It's not called cheating
If that person was never yours,
And you were never theirs.
It's called lying.
You lied and she lied
That you both were soul mates.

She became one of my worst fears.
She became my nightmares and tears.
She became long nights of whiskey.
My glasses are covered in pain and always misty.

Even a lonely moon
Is beautiful at night.

To Choose Her

All she wanted was to be chosen.
All you gave her was broken.

She wanted to love you and give you her all,
But you kept chipping away till you made her fall.

She fell and she fell until she could feel no more.
She turned into everything you hated, even a whore.

You can't blame her when you fucked her out of her life.
All you had to do was choose her and make her your wife.

My dear friends and family,
If I am to die today,
Do not let her attend my funeral.
Not that I will know.
But she is the one who took so many years from my life
By means of a broken heart.
If not for her,
We would not be here today.

No gesture at all mattered,
Trying to prove anything to you.
The only gesture that was important
I had taken way too long to do.

Then I finally jumped.
Finally, after so long, I took the chance.
But you looked at it and laughed
With your cold, hard glance.

I was too late.
Just like I have been so many times before.
I came up short once again.
You already had shut that door.

Alone I ate, and alone I drank
On your birthday today.
It was peaceful; it was quiet.
But it wasn't how I imagined this day.

Pondering my mistakes,
Recounting all my faults,
Wanting to find you and grab you.
My love for you I exalt.

Forgetting Lendzay Jons,
Like the movie except with her name.

It took him a week,
But it's taking me way longer.
Waiting for the pain to fade,
Waiting to become stronger.

Hoping to honestly laugh, maybe smile again,
And no longer needing to drink.
Let my mind become clear and steady.
My life is on its brink.

I'm dying, dear God.
My soul is slowly leaving its body.
Please bring her back to me
So my heart can dance again.

I Cried a Lot for You, Boo

Looked out towards the western skies
And asked him, "Why?"
My heart knew you were the one,
But to my heart he lied.

I cried and cried
Every single lonesome night
To bring you back to me,
And make everything once again right.

"It's Going to Be OK"

"It's going to be OK."
You keep telling yourself that.
You try to convince yourself
You'll laugh and smile about this down the road.
But you won't.
You will keep yourself busy throughout the day.
Then when night falls,
The memories will come back to you,
And it won't be OK.

It's your birthday today.
But I feel like it's the anniversary of a death
For I feel emptiness without you.

We always sat across from each other
When we should have sat close.
I wish I could go back to those times.
I miss them the most.

You cannot make someone fall in love with you again.
All you can do is remind them how you messed up.
If you can.
If you can get that chance again.

You never got the best version of me.
Now that I'm ready, you don't want me.
Was I ever something you wanted?
Was I never a love to be?

I got whiskey, and I got beer.
I got a heartache behind all these tears.
I drink and I smoke.
Smoking up so much dope.
Maybe it'll make you fade away.
Maybe it won't.
Maybe I'll never move on.
Maybe I'll never learn how to cope.

I want you to be happy forever.
I just wanted you to be happy forever with me.

I can't take back time.
Not the way it took me.

No other will ever touch my soul
How she touched it.

I never want to sleep again
Because there you are,
In my dreams,
Loving the shit out of me.

Listening to "These Days"
By a guy named Macklemore.
Reminded me of our love,
The joy and spirit to the core.

Then there was this line he sang
That I couldn't get out of my head.
Something about holding hands;
They'd laugh about the fun they had.

I then remembered when you sent me that.
It was almost a year ago.
I should have known that's when it was over,
And you were already ready to go.

She'll help the time pass
And keep the bedside warm.
But she'll never be you,
The women I mourn.

There are no number of days that it will take,
Take to forget you, my love.
There are no number of nights
That I won't pray to the man above,
Begging for you back.

Being rejected by you was fine
Because I was still getting something from you.
Even if it wasn't love,
It was something.

I never want to threaten your happiness again.
I just want you to know that I'm still in love with you.

I know who I was,
Someone I never want to be again.
A life of lies,
A life of hurt and sins.

I did you wrong
In so, so many ways.
I will feel shame and sorrow
For so, so many days.

There is no soul on this earth
That can say they don't have but one regret.
We all have one,
And we will take them with us to the afterlife.

The Loofah

When did I know it was over?
When she bought me shower supplies for Christmas.
He got Nikes.
I got shampoos, lotions, and a loofah.

"Stop Drinking," She Said

She asked me to stop drinking,
And I said, "I can't."
Not until she comes back.
I'll drink and drink till I see her shadows in the dark.
I'll drink till I die if I have to.
I'll drink as long as we're apart.

Bullshit

I read somewhere
That stories end, but love doesn't.
Bullshit.
My heart and the love it had died
The day you left.

Pour your heart into your purpose.
All of it at once.
Make sure she's worth it
Because loneliness sucks.

I'm a hopeless romantic.
I still believe in happy endings
And forever after.

I know our life wasn't real,
Like you told me so many times.
But it sure was one of the best make-believe stories ever.

I'd rather die with this broken-down heart
Than live a life where I never knew you.

I'd rather just say my head is aching
Than say my heart is broken.

What We Had

We had everything
But honesty and trust.
We had more deceit for each other,
And othering lust.

But the laughter and friendship
We definitely had.
We had bad timing, it seems.
We had love, hope, but were sad.

I couldn't let you love me
For I wasn't over her.
And I could never love you back
Because I needed to love me first.

I have everything?
I have everyone?
I have nothing
If I don't have you.

I begged and I pleaded,
"Please take us back. Please take us back."
I swore I'd never drop to my knees,
But I need to before this heart attack.

I could tell when you kissed me
You no longer missed me.

Those nights you said that you used to dream about me,
I could tell you dreamed of another.
It was just plain to see.

I went back and read the letters
That you once wrote.
I could reside in every word like a beautiful quote.

We always planned for our future,
But the future, it is no more.

I sat in the car this morning,
In the parking lot of a shopping center.
My hands in my face,
Crying like a child who's broken.
I know I need to snap out of it,
But I can't quite yet.
Hoping today might be the day.
But again, hoping for what?

Stuck in Love

You fall in love with a soul
That becomes a part of you.
They can do no wrong,
Though in all others' eyes,
That's all they do.
They're perfect,
The most perfect being in this world.
And yet they always strike you down with vengeance,
But you don't care to feel it.
Nothing fuckin' matters.
You're blind to anything else,
Blind to what is right.
And you fight to forget what is wrong.
You're stuck,
Stuck in love.

Printed in the United States
by Baker & Taylor Publisher Services